Jill — You're strength as a woman and as a human is unparalled. I hope this book reminds you of that when you don't feel that way. Thanks for all the times of infectious laughter.

Taryn

becoming.

Renaada Williams

you
were the definition
of what a man
father
and friend
should be.
you
always making something out of nothing possible
you taught me to be in tune with my feelings
but not to be overwhelmed.
you
taught me to be selfless
and to refrain
from treating people the way they treat me.
you
made sure my eyes were wide open
and ensured my heart was always pure.
there are no amount of thank yous
worthy enough
to explain the honor i feel
not only to have known you
but to be a portion of everything you were.
you
are the reason
i know happiness is not only possible
but achievable.

- i dedicate this to you
grandfather

thank you.

for believing in me.

dear beautiful soul

i know its hard
like
really hard
this thing called life
its
interesting
to say the least
i want you to know that
i believe in you
i want you to know that
you
are amazing
i know
that you are beautiful
i know a lot of times
family
friends
and all of the relationships in between
want you
to stay strong
i
want you to know
that its ok
if you cant be
but i pray
we
can find a way to
t o g e t h e r.

from here on out.

i knew that i could fly
well
at least i thought i could.
that was until
someone from the distance
yelled for me to get down
you'll hurt yourself
they said
but i knew if i let go
i would be alright
i knew that if i took the first step
id be soaring through the sky.
did you hear me? i said get down!
its as if i could feel them coming.
i knew they were upset
who was i to tell them
to let go
be brave
strong
and confident
who was i to tell them to believe?
after all
they've been here much longer than i have.
they've experienced things i'm still imagining.
so i decided
maybe they were right
and got down.

- dear adolescent
you are wrong

believing that you can fly
is only the beginning.

some say
if it doesn't hurt
it cant be love
but
if it does
you
shouldn't want it anyway

you
looked like everything
i ever wanted
beautiful brown eyes
nice smile
body soft
like sheepskin
i
was mistaken
when nighttime struck
your eyes lit up under the moon
you howled through the night
and only then did i realize
you
were pretending

- wolf in sheeps clothing

its funny how easily the monster in my head
can cuddle me softly while laying in my bed.

i realized i am nothing with you
even though
i
still
want to stay

i
am waiting at the end of the promise
you
forgot you made.

do you know what it feels like
to constantly get pushed out
while
being asked to stay?

only you
telling me
that i am beautiful
as if i've never heard it before
only you
to give me everything
i'm looking for
again.

- new bae

being with someone else
doesn't always symbolize
a new start.

i prayed
you
would be my one and only
and you were.
however
for her
you were the same

- the other woman

the problem wasn't
me
belonging to you
it was that
you
never belonged to me.

i
stayed longer
longer than i should have
trying to teach you how to love me
when
i
didn't even know
what that meant.

i
cried myself to sleep
while you
lay next to me
unbothered
unaware
and
uninterested

i tucked myself in again that night
and told myself
i didn't need a goodnight kiss
or empty i love yous
because dreams will be had
regardless of this nightmare.

the more i listen to myself
the closer i am to the truth.

trust the voice your gut is pulling from

- instincts

you
are the prettiest bouquet
of dying flowers
i
have ever seen.

i
like a fool
stayed
waiting for the day
you
would do something different

i
loved myself first
and even then
they
didn't love me back

we
have been back at square one
at least
one hundred
times already.

- starting over

don't stay
feeling sorry for me
i've been in so many pieces
enough times
to know
how to put myself together again.

- pity

attempting to make something whole
of two halves
isn't impossible
it just isn't common
with what
we
are doing

- broken hearts

i tried to forgive the lies you told
but
your smile
makes me remember

- trust issues

i expected you to fix me
failing to realize
soon after
you left
i
would still be broken

and
the main reason i left
was because
you
expected me to stay

here i am
loving something so deeply
and desperately
wanting it back
although
if i had it
i wouldn't have known
what to do with it anyway

you
missing me more than you have ever loved me.

- irony

go ahead
talk about me
in the worst way imaginable.
just try to forgive yourself
afterwards.

i'm sorry
sounds a lot like
forgive me
but,
its really meant to mean
ill do it again.

and
not only is it harder
its pretty impossible to forgive someone
who expects to be forgiven again.

i decided
i didn't want to be a pawn anymore
but
how else would i *win*
if i didn't sacrifice
pieces of myself.

- love in the name of chess

because what did love feel like
if it wasn't abuse anyway

when you left
i didn't cry
because i was *broken*
i cried
because i **survived**
you
tried to leave pieces of me
scattered
in places id never think to check
but
i
discovered them anyway
beneath tear stained pillowcases we slept on
the morning mug
you often placed your lips on
in the shower
as suds replaced your kisses
and
in my heart
where most of them remained
because scattered or not
they didn't belong to you
and
they would have found their way back to me
anyway.

belive me
i will go on living
as i was
before we met
i
will not allow this
to make me feel
as though i cant

there are
pieces of me
living within people who once held my heart
pieces of me
that i never want back
not because i need them to feel whole
but
because i gave them away so someone else could.

and when it was over
i came up gasping for air
as if
i've forgotten how to breathe

- the breakup

love
changed me
it made me feel
like
i
should be second
it made me forget
i
had needs
it made me
compromise myself
and ultimately
it
broke
my
heart

you told me to swallow my tongue
not literally of course
but you made it impossible
to speak
without being interrupted
without sounding like i was not smart enough
without ever feeling like you were listening
and so,
i ate it.

you
let the *perception* of love
abuse you
after
raising
nurturing
and most times
stepping completely outside of your being
simply handing yourself over
all because
you believed
you found it

and just like that
e v e r y t h i n g
about you suddenly changed
the way you looked
the way you talked
and even your actions
because
i
no longer cared.

me
attracting people that need me
but don't know how to treat me
simply because
i
haven't stayed consistent
and faithful
to myself
long enough
to be found
by someone that does.

treating someone the way they treated you
doesn't prove how badly you were hurt
instead,
it'll prove how long it takes for you to heal.

you
do not feel this bad on your own.
learn to hold people accountable for how
they make you feel.

everyone loves to talk about a sad woman
as if she
doesn't have a journey
a message
as if she
isn't a walking testimony
as if she
will never be happy again.

and
if your heart says feel everything,
thats **EXACTLY** what you do.

being broken is a matter of opinion

you
attracting people that need you
but
don't know how to treat you
simply because
you
haven't stayed consistent
and faithful
to yourself
long enough to be found
by someone that does.

i don't want to remember the pain
h o w e v e r
i also don't want to forget

never stop talking about your journey
there will be people who don't understand that
it isn't about *wanting* to stay hurt
its always about trying to figure out how not to be.

it was hard
understanding that
eventually
it would stop
eventually
it wouldn't be
so cold
i
knew it would be beautiful
but somehow
it seemed like
it
would never end.

- the coldest winter

i
am not allowed
to call myself different
when theres a word
for what i *have*.

- depression

i kept going
not because i wanted to
trust me,
all of me wanted to stop.
i kept going
because i deserved to know
what not giving up on myself felt like.

your love
cut so deep
pain sharp
like a stencil
against my body
to trace over

- infliction

i
felt like i died
at least
a million times before

- modern day feline

i do the best i can
helping everyone i know
become better
while
they
stand around
and watch me
become worse

its rarely a discussion
we aren't talking about it as much as we should
however
when someone who suffers *within* mental illness dies
and you
have to show up for a funeral
or you
cant believe it actually happened
or when they
are floating around the internet
in pictures
in videos
in memories
you care.
right?

and
i've convinced myself
that no one
would want to be with someone
so sad
like me
anyway

- idle mind

don't try to get into my head
and make me believe
the solution
is in this capsule
as if all of these years
i've spent
living
thinking
and feeling
could be fixed that easily

- zoloft

as if talking aloud to someone
that tells me everything i tell myself
when i have a clear spot in my brain
will make the clutter in my brain
just magically clean itself up
but
i went anyway
and
i sat across from a woman
that seemed so pleasant and eager to help
i kept going back
because
i guess thats what i was *supposed* to be doing
but
what exactly is she *supposed* to be doing?
what are these pills *SUPPOSED* to be doing?
because
whenever i have idle time
i'm reminding myself that i don't have nine lives
and
if i try again i might actually strike out.
i might actually end up tear stained
makeup smothered
on a cold corpse that no longer looks anything like me
because
dying seemed to be the only thing that made sense to me
however
i went again anyway.

she looked at me
with love in her heart
pain in her voice
and defeat in her eyes
and in that moment
i knew
i wouldn't be going back

- therapy sessions

to wake up everyday
telling myself
i feel like living today
as if it were that easy
as if i didn't fight this hard for today
yesterday.
as if i didn't break every bone in my body
bending and molding
to fit inside places
i probably shouldn't have been in.
haven't we all
had our last straw?
questions to a higher power
trying to figure out what went wrong
i know you know what it feels like
to not be able
to breathe
to speak
to feel
i know
what hands clenched to chest from crying all night feels like
and
i know
that you do too

- normal

there is love out here for me.

there is n o t h i n g more powerful than us
black kings and queens
we
are the only ones acting like there is

to see
people
develop so much love to be everything like us
but
the color of our skins

- the power of melanin gods

theres people out here
who would rather see you
hurt
struggling
and
suffering
leave them where they are
and say
nothing.

we
are worth much more
than
t-shirts
headlines
street names
and
#hashtags

i
need
more people
who look like
me
to make it!

no
i
didn't have to stand around
and watch someone i love
dangle from a tree
to know
theres people out here
that still think
we
are disposable

i
wont apologize
to the people that don't know my struggle
they will never endure my pain.
they do not understand
my journey
but they will always
be able to hear about it
as long as
i
am able
to write about it.

as if
killing us off
isn't killing us internally
as if
walking around
trying to make it back home
isn't a mission
as if coming outside
wanting
to go outside
isn't a mission.

and they thought
letting you out
meant
you
had justice
as if
that
ever.
gave you
peace

- Kalief Browder

we
have the right to remain silent
but God forbid we speak.

i just want to live in a world
that i'm not afraid
to be
alive in.

there isn't anything redeemable
about hate
but,
how powerful we must be
to have it remain infinite for us.

be brave
be bold
and
remain beautiful
no matter how bad you feel

our time isn't coming
its already here.

there is
nothing
more complicated
than not knowing
what you want
and
accepting everything else
that just doesn't seem
worth it

- meantime

you
are not here to be
everything
for someone else
and
nothing
for self.

blessings
mean more to some
than praying does
either way
im thankful

- priorities

you
are not this strong
to be weak
for someone else.

there is
so much beauty
in
growth
change
and
practice.

- pursuit

it will not happen overnight
it may take days
months
or even years
but in the end
i promise it'll be worth it.

my journey
was sought out
planted
and fertilized
for this growth.

don't spend all of your time and energy
giving someone else your life
share yourself in portions
enough to have some for them
enough to still hold onto you.

the thing about art
about magic
is that some people will get it
it'll move them in ways they could never even imagine
and for some
they wont understand
they'll have more reasons than a few
to make it seem as though
this
as though
you
aren't as beautiful
and powerful
aren't as *realistic* as they would want you to be
and you
have to know
you don't require an explanation.

understand that being strong is beautiful
but
so is vulnerability.

soon you will be
trying to find
anything
to break the fall you feel
while
staring at your reflection in the mirror
knowing
love
never
felt that real

- self love

create your own meaning
understand what feels good to you
recognize
what doesn't
don't give in
this
is not it.
love
is not meant to be
this exhausting.

you
have to stop customizing yourself
to fit someone who doesn't even deserve
you.

choose
yourself
your faith
your intuition
every.
singlc.
time.

- never give up

i
was never looking for the light
at the end of the tunnel
i
didn't go into the mouth of the beast
thinking
it would be something pretty
left over for me to grasp
i knew inside there was a jungle
i knew i had to be
hungry enough
strong enough
and passionate enough
to survive

we are created in the darkness
and
forced into light

- new life

remind yourself
to be more specific when you pray
you
cannot ask to be used by God
and be mad
when
you
are tested

nobody
will ever be what you need
if you
are still learning
what that is

- acceptance

we are staying in unsafe places
on purpose
and blaming other people for breaking our hearts.

stop saying
i'm fine
when you're not
its okay
to say nothing
when
n o t h i n g
is how you feel.

you
are allowed to detour
as many times as you want
as long as you find your way back
to self.

you
are the only one
not putting yourself first

you owe it to yourself
to be by yourself
to love
and value yourself
to understand that you need time,
time to know
what you will
and will not tolerate.

silence is important
being still is important
taking the control back
over your mind
over your body
over your energy
is important.

pay them no mind
when they say
you aren't good enough.
only a fool can hold
a diamond
in their bare hand
and not be amazed.

be
so full of
love
trust
positivity
respect
magic
life
and honor
for self.
that you just naturally ward off anything less.

i am.
chanting and drilling
beautiful words
into my mind.
into my heart.
into my soul.
because,
if i am not telling myself that
i am.
i'm allowing myself to say that i am not.

you
are worth
everything beautiful you thought you weren't
and growing out of all the things
that made you feel that way in the first place.

never forget
to pick up the pieces
no matter
how old
or useless
they may seem
they
will still create
a
masterpiece.

- to all the broken hearts

you
have to be the light for yourself
even when nobody else can see it.

don't wait another minute
to do something that makes your soul sing.

this
is not only in my words
but my actions
this
is in the way that i speak
and
the way that i address
e v e r y t h i n g
this
is waking up everyday in my purpose
and
sharing it
with you.

someones definition
of a disaster
will create
amazing poetry.
w r i t e t h r o u g h i t.

i didn't always believe myself when i told myself
i love you
its something that i'm no longer ashamed of
everyone was always telling me how to love
telling me id be incapable of giving
or
receiving it
until i loved myself so deeply it glowed brighter than the moon
but
i am standing here unashamed
to let you know i've had my share of doubt
id look in the mirror and see right through myself
i cut lines upon my legs so precise
to the point that i knew exactly where my jeans would stop.
i wasn't really trying to go
i didn't really *want* to die.
i wanted so badly to shake this thing they called the "*the black dog*"
all the while asking myself why
everything
negative
depressing
and
downright wrong *had* to be black?
however
looking at my reflection . . .
actually seeing how beautifully brown and black i was
i didn't have to know the face of *love* to glow
because i did a damn good job at exuding it.
i had to tell myself that a dog
is one of the most
loyal
caring
forgiving
loving
and nurturing animals ever!
it made me realize why my heart was so big.
why i would literally go naked just so someone would have clothes
hungry so that someone else would have food
and id be damned
if i didn't go broke
ensuring that someone else didn't go without help.
so if *that* makes me *"the black dog"*
so be it!
i don't need anyone to tell me about love.
because on this journey i discovered
that life is challenging
scary
it can get hard
cloudy
and lonely.
however
i love myself enough to know that i am stronger today
than i ever was before.

becoming.

i believe in every single thing you stand for.
i believe in your spirit
i believe in your strength
i believe in your journey
and i believe that whatever you put fourth the effort to achieve
you
will do that and then some!
i love you on purpose
and don't you
ever
forget that.

everyday
for the rest of your life
remember
you
are loved
you
are brilliant
you
are beautiful
you
are resilient
you
are protected
you
are loving
you
are worthy
you
are
m a g i c !

- claim it

i promise to carry you in my heart first
but
forever in my soul.
you
are the reason this is possible

dear beautiful reader
thank you

until next time, thank you for believing in me.
@renaadawilliams

Made in the USA
Middletown, DE
28 November 2018